Science

Chapter 1

The Science Fair Topic

Mia and Bailee looked forward to this year's Lakeview Elementary School (LES) Science Fair. The girls enjoyed most of the subjects that were taught at their school, however, they both expressed that Science was their favorite subject of them all. Their science teacher, Mr. Watt, made learning about the basics of biology, chemistry and physics fun. He showed the kids how to create electrical circuits by using a battery, wires and a light bulb or demonstrating how a clay volcano erupts by pouring vinegar over baking soda. Science class was the only place you can make a big mess in school and not get in trouble. It was all part of the experimentation and observations tested.

This year was the third time Mia and Bailee entered a project into the LES Science Fair. Previously, they demonstrated how the amount of air pressure inflated into a ball, influenced how high it bounces; how a liquid, such as milk, has a different surface tension than water; methods of creating a rainbow using a compact disc; how a color wheel, with primary colors, appears white as it spins at a high rate of speed and the sisters built a model of the solar system. Each year was a new challenge, trying to choose a project that would be different than the others. And this year was no different. The sisters were up to the challenge.

Mia and Bailee sat at the dinner table trying to decide what their next science project will be. "I really want to show something cool!" said Bailee. "I agree. We need something unique that other kids won't think of," replied Mia. The sisters searched on the computer for science projects, but there wasn't one that seemed to excite them. "What are we going to do? We need to submit our topic tomorrow," said Bailee

As they scrolled through numerous science fair ideas, one topic stood out from the rest. "Wait! I found our topic," said Mia. "What is it?" replied Bailee. "FINGERPRINTS," said Mia. "Dad works as a Fingerprint Examiner. He can help us demonstrate how no two people have the same fingerprints and how to make an invisible fingerprint visible," continued Mia. "Good idea Mia. I'm going to tell dad our idea," said Bailee. "Hey, it was my idea!" muttered Mia. "I'll race you," said Bailee. The sisters ran in different directions, eagerly to reach their dad in the garage. Mia and Bailee burst into the opened garage breathless. "I won!" said a winded Bailee. "What are you girls doing?"

asked Dad. "We decided on a topic for this year's science fair and raced to find you," replied Bailee. "I came up with the idea. Can I tell dad?" asked Mia. "Sure Sis," replied Bailee. "We are going to exhibit, The Science of Fingerprints. You can help us make a display and show everyone some of the things you do at work," said Mia. "That's a great idea girls. We'll work together to make this the best project in the fair," replied Dad. The sisters "high fived" each other and excitedly ran up to the kitchen to see their mom. "Mom, can you help us fill out our science fair entry form? We have our topic and it is due tomorrow," said Bailee. "Sure," replied Mom. The form was filled out and placed in Mia's backpack. "Sounds like a fun project. Don't forget to turn it in," said Mom. Mia and Bailee went back to the family computer and began to outline their display. "I feel like that crime solver that we read about in the "Kid Detective Violet Riddle" book series," said Mia. "Maybe we can use fingerprints to solve a crime ourselves," said a giggling Bailee.

Science class was the only place you can make a big mess in school and not get in trouble.

Chapter 2

The Jelly Bean Contest

The Lakeview Elementary School students climbed off their buses and proceeded into the building for another fun filled day of learning. Before heading to their classrooms, Mia and Bailee dashed toward the main office. A table was placed next to the office entrance door with a box that read "Science Fair Entry Forms".   Mia opened the box and placed their entry inside. "Let's go Mia. We'll be late," said an anxious Bailee. As the girls scurried to their assigned hallways, Mia yelled "Bye Bailee!"

Mrs. Rogers asked the students to take their seats and begin the day. She called out everyone's name and recorded the class attendance. Just as Mrs. Rogers reached Mia Panari, she rushed into the room. "Sorry Mrs. Rogers. I won't be late again," said a reserved Mia. "That's OK. You have never been late before and I know it won't be a habit," replied Mrs. Rogers. Mia blushed and sat at her desk. "Did you enter the Science Fair?" whispered her friend Michele. "Bailee and I just placed our entry form in the box," replied Mia. "What is your topic?" asked Michele. "I don't want to tell anyone yet. It will be a surprise," said Mia trying to speak softly. Mrs. Rogers gave a stern stare towards the girls and continued to discuss the morning topic. The girls immediately opened their books and intently listened to the lesson.

"Good Morning," said Principal Gildman over the intercom. "I thought we would begin our school day with an exciting announcement. A jar filled with jelly beans has been placed on a table in the cafeteria. The student who guesses the correct amount of jelly beans will receive 3 homework passes for the year and keep the entire jar of candy. Each class will have an opportunity to participate. Mrs. Fair, the school guidance counselor, will sit at the table to insure proper contribution. Good luck all. Have a great day," concluded Mr. Gildman.

A chorus of cheerful student voices began to fill the school hallways, as they were anxious to get to the cafeteria and take part in the jelly bean contest. The teachers momentarily regained order in their classrooms and continued their lessons.

In Mrs. Lerner's class, Bailee whispered to Emma, "It's almost time. We're one of the first classes to go to lunch. Try to get to the front of the line." At that moment, the bell rang and it was time for lunch. Bailee, Emma and Jackie sprang from their chairs, grabbed their lunches and headed to the classroom door. "Everyone slow down. I know you're excited and eager to go to the cafeteria. But, we don't need anyone to get hurt and everyone will get a chance to participate," said Mrs. Lerner.

The students formed an orderly line and proceeded to lunch. Mrs. Fair announced, as everyone enjoyed their lunch, she would call each table of children up to the jelly bean jar. The first group was asked to come up and guess.

Hastily, an impatient boy rushed to the front of the line and banged into the table. The jar of jelly beans teetered back and forth on the table. The cafeteria was filled with a loud gasp. "Oh No! It's going to fall!" said a panicked Jackie. Immediately, Mrs. Fair grabbed the jar and steadied it. The students clapped knowing that the ultimate prize was safe.

The embarrassed boy sat on the floor wishing that he was invisible. Mrs. Lerner helped Stan Mosby up and walked him to the lobby. After being spoken to, the young boy was allowed to participate in the contest in a calm and orderly manner. Stan slunk back into the cafeteria and glared at the annoyed students staring at him. Stan Mosby was 10 years old, a bit hyperactive, difficult to deal with in class and always seemed to find trouble. As a result, he did not have many friends to play with due to his recklessness.

A few minutes passed and Bailee's table was called. "Wow!" said Bailee. "That sure is a lot of jelly beans." She gazed at the array of colorful candy, wrote down her best guess and placed it in a box. Throughout the afternoon, the rest of the school took part in the challenge.

Mia met Bailee, as they boarded the school bus to go home. "Did you enter the jelly bean contest Mia?" asked Bailee. "Yes. I couldn't believe how many there were," replied Mia. "How many did you guess?" asked Bailee. "383. How many did you say?" asked Mia. "402," replied Bailee. Bailee told Mia what Stan Mosby did while she was in the cafeteria. "I'm glad Mr. Fair was quick enough to catch the jelly bean jar. That would have been a disaster," said Mia. "And Stan would have had the whole school furious at his actions," replied Bailee.

The embarrassed boy sat on the floor
wishing that he was invisible.

<h1 align="center">Chapter 3</h1>

Frolicking Comet

Mia and Bailee where greeted off the bus by their mom. "How was your day girls?" asked Mom. "Fun. We're having a jelly bean contest. The person who guesses the correct amount gets 3 homework passes and the entire jar," replied Bailee. "Sounds great! I better call the dentist," said a joking Mom. Both girls giggled. "Why don't you two go relax and I'll make you a snack," said Mom.

Mia and Bailee changed into comfortable play clothes and met in the kitchen. Their mom prepared a medley of fruit slices, cheese and crackers. "Thanks mom. I'm starving," said Mia. Bailee shook her head in agreement, as she was unable to speak with a mouthful of cheese.

Mia and Bailee finished their tasty snacks and went outside to play. "Let's play catch with your softball Mia," said Bailee. "Ok. I'll get the gloves," replied Mia. The girls began tossing the ball back and forth. Mia played third base in the Gaitsville Recreation League. She has shown a strong arm, as well as, a very good eye at the plate. "Not too hard Mia," said Bailee. "I can't catch as well as you do." Mia liked to show her sister how far and accurate she could throw. The girls stood approximately 65 feet away from each other. Mia wound up and hurled the softball toward Bailee. The ball flew through the air rapidly and stuck in Bailee's glove as she held her hand up high. "Nice throw Mia," said Bailee. Bailee tossed the ball back towards Mia, but it was misdirected and rolled under a bush in the neighbor's yard. As Mia walked to retrieve it, she saw Comet frolicking over to the ball. "Hurry Mia!" yelled Bailee. "Comet is going to take the ball." Mia's calm walk turned into a sprint and a race against Comet. Just as she was within a foot of reaching the ball, Comet sprung forward and grabbed the ball in her mouth. She leapt backwards and dashed around the Panari's yard.

Mia and Bailee chased Comet throughout the yard. Twisting and turning around the playscape, jumping through flower gardens while lunging to grab the ball. The girls knew Comet was only having fun. She always managed to get loose from the Somersby's yard and play with Mia and Bailee. Following a few minutes of eluding the girls, Comet sat in the grass and dropped the ball. "Finally," said Mia, as she was trying to catch her breath.

The girls heard Mr. Somersby calling Comet. The energetic dog sprang from the ground and sprinted back to her house. "Grose, the ball is all slimy," said Bailee. "Next time we play catch, we need to keep an eye out for that crazy dog," said a smiling Mia.

At that moment, Mr. Panari arrived home from work. He drove into the driveway and honked the car horn. Mia and Bailee ran over to see what was so important. "Wait until you see the supplies that I brought home for your science fair project," said Dad. The girls were wide eyed and eager to see what was in the bags. Each girl grabbed a bag and brought them into the house. Their dad began to remove the supplies and place them on the dining room table. There were pictures of each type of fingerprint pattern, a timeline showing the history of fingerprint identification and a chart demonstrating how two fingerprints are compared. "What are these?" asked Bailee. "That is a jar of black fingerprint powder and a fingerprint brush. Not only can you discuss the science of fingerprints, but everyone will be amazed when you physically develop an invisible fingerprint on a piece of glass," said an excited Dad. "Can you show us?" asked Mia. "Sure," replied Dad.

Their mom overheard the conversation and joined everyone in the dining room. "This looks interesting, but please don't make a mess in here," said Mom. "Good idea. This may get messy, so let's take this to the garage," said Dad. Mr. Panari placed a piece of glass on the workbench and touched it with his finger. Then he sprinkled some of the black powder on a piece of paper and gently dipped the bristles of the brush into the powder. As he gently sweeping across the surface of the glass, a visible fingerprint appeared. "Wow!" said the girls. "No one is going to do this at the fair," exclaimed Mia.

"The science fair is tomorrow. So, why don't you work on gluing the pictures to the display board," said Mom. That night, the sisters worked hard on their project and were satisfied with their accomplishment.

"Hurry Mia!" called Bailee. "Comet is going to take the ball."

Chapter 4

Science Fair

At the conclusion of another fun day at school, Lakeview Elementary was bustling with lively children preparing to demonstrate their science fair projects. Shortly afterwards, the parking lot was filled with parents arriving with their child's projects. The gymnasium was set up with several tables, which had been designated with the appropriate grade level and teacher.

Mia and Bailee met their mom in the lobby of the school and helped her carry the project materials to the gym. "There's our table," said Mia. The sisters entered the science fair together and used Mia's grade level to demonstrate the project. "Hello girls. Do you need help arranging your display on the table?" asked Mrs. Rogers. "No thank you," said Bailee. Mia propped up the display board, which showed all the pictures that their dad provided them with from his work. The display read "The Science of Fingerprints". Then Bailee removed two pieces of clear plastic, black fingerprint powder, a fingerprint brush and gloves. She organized these materials on the table, in front of the display. It was not only required to stay within your designated space on the table, but polite so others can have space as well.

The science fair began with a few remarks from the school principal. "Welcome everyone to this year's science fair. This wonderful event is always a great way for the students to show their creativity and vision for science. Please move throughout the room and observe the many fascinating projects," said Principal Gildman.

The gymnasium was filled with parents attentively listening to the students explaining their projects. There were erupting volcanos, electrical cars, hover crafts, solar systems and numerous others.

Mia and Bailee had a group of parents inquiring about their

display. Mia began by explaining that fingerprints are unique to everyone. No two people have the same fingerprint arrangement in the entire world. Not even identical twins. She continued to demonstrate this fact by pointing out the unique features in the enlarged fingerprint photograph.

Next, Bailee's task was to demonstrate how an invisible fingerprint, known as latent, could be developed by applying black fingerprint powder. She asked one of the parents to place their finger on the clear piece of plastic. Then Bailee sprinkled some of the black powder on a piece of paper next to the plastic and gently dipped the bristles of the brush into the powder. As she gently sweeping across the surface of the plastic, a visible fingerprint appeared. "Wow!"

said the crowd gathered in front of the display. Mia concluded by saying, "Once a fingerprint is made visible, it can be compared to someone and determined to be them or not." The observing parents thanked Mia and Bailee for their demonstration and moved around the room. Mr. and Mrs. Panari stood by the girl's project listening to their explanation of the science of fingerprints. "We are so proud of you both. What a wonderful job you did," said Mom. "I couldn't have explained it better," exclaimed Dad.

Unexpectedly, there was a stir of activity at the end of the gym. "Stan Mosby. What is he going to do?" asked a worried Bailee. Stan lined up three bottles of soda on the floor, and placed two Mentos mints into each. The reaction between the carbonated beverage and the Mentos mints caused the soda to erupt out of the bottles. Students gathered to see the array of soda geysers, which drenched the gym floor and surrounding walls. "What is going on?" asked Mr. Gildman. The principal reached the end of the room only to see a sticky, wet mess everywhere.

Stan Mosby was laughing at his antics and attempted to slink out of the building. "Stop!" yelled Mr. Gildman. A few parents, who stood by the door, grabbed Stan and held him for the principal. "What in the heavens are you thinking about?" asked an irritated Mr. Gildman. Stan just stood there with no answer. "You have made an enormous mess and you are going to learn to be responsible for your rude behavior. You're going to stay and help the school custodian clean all this up, no matter how long it takes. While you are doing that, I am going to have a chat with your parents," said Principal Gildman.

The lively gymnasium was as quiet as a church service. "Sorry for the inconvenience everyone. Please go back to the science fair and enjoy the student's hard-working efforts. "Stan Mosby is nothing but trouble," said Mia. "He's always trying to ruin everything," she continued. As the fair concluded, Mrs. Rogers announced that all projects will remain in the gymnasium so the school can have the opportunity to view them during the day. The crowd of students and parents proceeded out of the building leaving an annoyed Stan Mosby behind to clean up. Some students even scowled at him in disgust.

"That was a nice evening," said Mrs. Panari. "Up to the point of the soda geysers," replied Bailee. "Well, I think that everyone that participated did a wonderful job. We are proud of you both," said their Dad.

The reaction between the carbonated beverage and the Mentos mints caused the soda to erupt out of the bottles.

Chapter 5

The Missing Jelly Bean Jar

It was a gloomy, rainy morning as Mia and Bailee gathered their backpacks and proceeded to the bus. Their mom stood on the front lawn and waved to the two girls as the school bus drove down the street. All the way to school, the bus was filled with chatter about the disaster Stan Mosby caused at last night's science fair. "You should have been there," Mia said to her friend Michele. "Stan made a huge mess and Mr. Gildman was furious," she continued. "What did Mr. Gildman do to him?" asked Michele. "He made Stan stay and help the school custodian clean up the mess that he created," answered Mia.

The bus reached the school and the students proceeded to their classrooms. As the herd of rain drenched children entered LES, Stan Mosby could be seen mopping the wet floor as they passed by. He gave a scowl to anyone that looked at him. Stan's punishment was agreed upon by his parents and Mr. Gildman. He was allowed to proceed to his classroom after the floor was dry and no one was arriving off the buses. "I hope you learned your lesson," said Principal Gildman. "You can go to your class now. Enjoy the day Stan," he continued.

The morning announcements bellowed over the intercom. "The winner of the jelly bean contest will be announced at 1:00 p.m. today. You may pick up the oversized prize in the art room," said Mrs. Fair. The classrooms began to get a bit stirred up, but the teachers quickly gained control and began their daily lessons.

Bailee looked at her schedule for the day and realized that she had art class at 10:20 a.m. Mrs. Lerner walked her class to the art room where they were met by Ms. Pastel. "Everyone take a seat at an easel. We are going to paint the object standing in the center of the room," said Ms. Pastel. The only thing the students saw was a tall object covered with a sheet. Ms. Pastel walked over and pulled the sheet off, revealing a 5 foot tall stuffed giraffe wearing yellow sunglasses. The children burst out laughing. "Everyone remember to use the simple shapes and feature tools which we covered last week. You may use crayons, markers or paint, but I encourage you to start your drawings with a pencil. Have fun," said Ms. Pastel.

Bailee sketched her giraffe with a pencil then added purple patches using paint. "I'm naming my giraffe Sprinkles," said Bailee. The children sitting nearby giggled. "Everyone is doing a wonderful job. We have some brown giraffes, grey ones and even a purple giraffe," said a smiling Ms. Patel.

While Bailee was waiting for the others to finish their drawings, she raised her hand and asked Ms. Pastel where the jar of jelly beans was. "We placed it on that window shelf and covered it with a towel," replied Ms. Pastel. "Can we see it?" asked Bailee's friend Emma. "Sure. The winner has already been decided anyway," replied Ms. Pastel. The comical teacher walked over to the window shelf and removed the towel from the jar. Ms. Pastel let out a gasp. "The jelly bean jar is gone!" she shrieked. In place of the jar was a cardboard box.

At that moment, the bell rang which signaled the end of class. Ms. Pastel hurried to the main office to inform Principal Gildman

what has happened. Immediately,
a broadcast bellowed throughout
the school. "We had an unfortunate
occurrence and the announcement
of the jelly bean contest winner will
be postponed. It has come to my
attention that the jelly bean jar is
missing from the art room. An
update will be forthcoming," said a
frustrated Mr. Gildman.

Ms. Pastel let out a gasp. "The jelly bean jar
is gone!" she shrieked.

Chapter 6

The Suspicious Fingerprints

As the disappointed students passed throughout the hallways, Mia yelled to Bailee and waved her over. "I wonder what happened to the jar," said Mia. "Our class was in the art room when Ms. Pastel discovered it missing," replied Bailee. "Let's go in the art room and you can show me where it was," said Mia. Bailee half-heartedly agreed.

The girls peeked in the art room and saw that no one was in there. "I'm nervous Mia. We're not supposed to be in here," said Bailee. "It's ok. We'll be quick," replied Mia. They scurried inside the room and headed to the window shelf. "See, whoever took the jar replaced it with this box," said Bailee. "What are those red marks on the box?" asked Mia. "Those look like fingerprints," replied Bailee. "Your right, just like our science fair project," exclaimed Mia. "I wonder what the red material is though," she continued. The girls looked on the rug near the shelf and noticed that someone spilled red paint. "I bet whoever spilled that paint had it on their hands and touched this box," said an inquisitive Bailee. Mia looked at Bailee with a smile. "I'm going to cut an area off the box with fingerprints, then we better get out of here," said Mia

The girls opened the art room door and dashed to their class-rooms. It was recess time and an opportunity for Mia and Bailee to discuss the jelly bean caper.

"This is exciting. We are going to solve the caper of the jelly beans by using fingerprints," said an eager Mia. "Just like Kid Detective Violet Riddle in those mystery books," replied Bailee. As the sisters were chatting, their friends, Michelle, Olivia, Emma and Jackie came over to invite them to play kickball.

The kickball game was a rematch between Bailee and her friends against Mia and her friends. The younger girls previously won at the Panari's house. Emma kicked the ball over third base and it bounced off a boy standing by the bushes. Mia began to race over and retrieve the ball but, Stan Mosby had already tossed it back. As she picked the ball up, Mia noticed red paint on the kickball. "That's strange," thought Mia. Then she remember-ed the spilled red paint in the art room. Mia began to get a bit uneasy realizing what she may have discovered.

"Time out!" yelled Mia. She raced over to Bailee, who was up next, and told her what she noticed. Bailee had a surprised look on her face as she realized what it meant. "Bai, kick the ball near Stan Mosby. I have a suspicion and want to see if it is true," said Mia. Bailee struck the ball and launched it over Olivia's head. Once again, it bounced off Stan Mosby. Stan glared at the girls and appeared annoyed that he was hit with the ball again. Mia feverishly sprinted to the ball. She grabbed it from Stan and noticed red paint on his pants and sneakers. "Just as I suspected," thought Mia.

The bell rang and ended recess. Mia filled Bailee in on the additional clues she discovered in the jelly bean caper. "We need to speak to dad tonight about the clues that we discovered today," said Bailee.

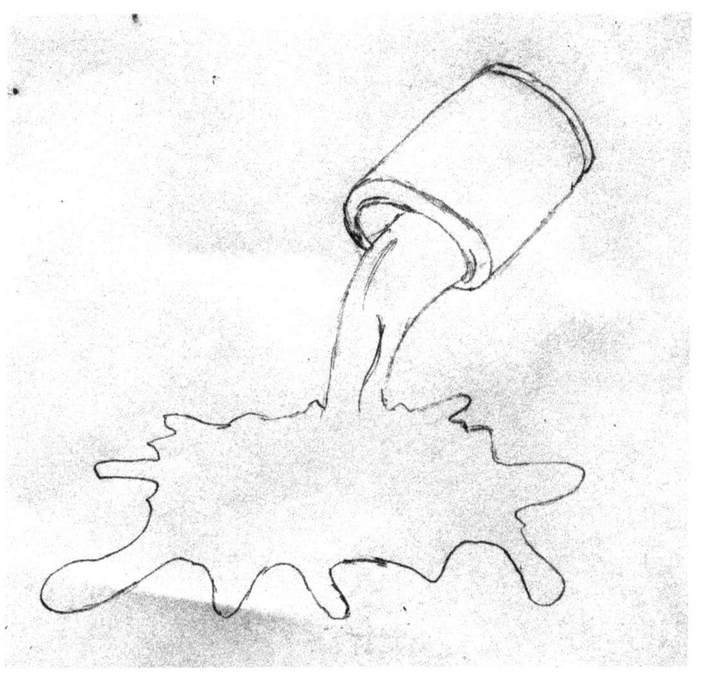

"I bet whoever spilled that paint had it on their hands and touched this box," said an inquisitive Bailee.

Chapter 7

Mia and Bailee Crack the Case

As the Panari's sat down together for dinner, Bailee began to tell their mom and dad about the incident in the art room. Mia continued and spoke about the clues which they had found. "Clue one: The red fingerprints on the box which was put in place of the jar. Clue two: The spilled red paint on the floor next to the window step. Clue three: The red paint on Stan Mosby's hands, pants and sneakers.

Mr. and Mrs. Panari were speechless. "Very impressive, it sounds like you girls are young detectives and hot on the suspects trail," said Dad. "We are very close to solving this caper and need your help dad," exclaimed Bailee. "How can I say no, anything for my girls," said a smiling Dad. "We learned a lot from our science fair project and want to catch the culprit by identifying him through his fingerprints," said a determined Mia. "I think you already have," replied Dad, as he picked up the phone. "What did dad mean by that?" said Bailee.

Mr. Panari called Principal Gildman and filled him in on the clues which Mia and Bailee had found. Mr. Gildman was astonished by the observations and cleverness the girls displayed. "Your principal will take it from here girls," said Dad.

The next morning, Mia and Bailee were eager to get to school and see the jelly bean culprit identified. When they arrived at Lakeview Elementary, the girls walked past the main office and saw Stan Mosby, accompanied by his parents, Principal Gildman and Mrs. Fair. Mr. Gildman saw Mia and Bailee passing by and gave a wink.

Stan was presented with the facts of the present situation by the principal. "First, the jelly bean jar was taken and replaced by a cardboard box. Second, a container of red paint was hastily spilled on the floor next to the window step. Third, visible fingerprints in red paint were observed on the box. Our guess is that whoever took the jar, spilled the paint, transferred some on their hands and touched the box. Additionally, you had noticeable red paint splattered on your pants and shoes yesterday." Stan looked shocked at the amount of evidence that was linking him to the incident.

"Now, you can either admit that you took the jelly bean jar or we can simply have your fingerprints compared to the ones on the cardboard box," said a stern

Mr. Gildman. Stan's shoulders slunk down and he realized that he had been caught "Red Handed". "Where is the jelly bean jar, Stan?" asked Mrs. Fair. "I placed it in the custodian closet by the gym," replied Stan.

Mr. Gildman discussed the appropriate consequence with Mr. and Mrs. Mosby. As this was occurring, Mrs. Fair retrieved the jelly bean jar from the custodian closet. To her amazement, it did not seem to be opened.

The school intercom buzzed, as an announcement was about to be made by Principal Gildman. "Good morning students and faculty. Through a remarkable display of observation, we were able to locate the missing jelly bean jar. As such, I am proud to announce that the contest winner is

Bailee Panari." Mrs. Lerner's classroom erupted in cheers and Bailee was "high fived" by her friends Emma and Jackie. "You may go to the office and pick up your prize," said a smiling Mrs. Lerner.

Bailee walked down the hall, past the main office and continued to Mrs. Roger's classroom. She knocked on the door and asked if it would be alright to have Mia accompany her to pick up the jelly bean jar. Mrs. Rogers, who was aware of the sister's accomplishments, said it was fine. "Why do you need me to come with you Bai?" asked Mia. "I may have guessed the closest number of jelly beans, but without you, we would have never found out who the bandit was," said Bailee. Mia smiled and put her arm around

Bailee. "We did it together. Sisters Now. Sisters Always. Sisters Forever," said Mia.

"We did it together. Sisters Now. Sisters Always. Sisters Forever," said Mia.

The Sister Pact Adventures are dedicated to my wife and daughters who were the inspiration for these stories.

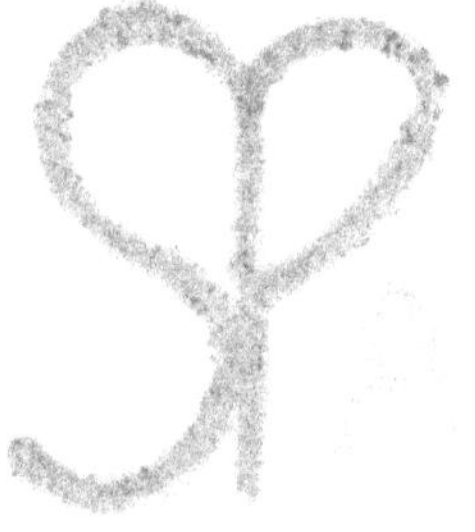

About The Author

K.M. Parisi has been published in scientific publications as a result of his professional career. However, one of his hobbies includes writing children books and incorporating some of his family's experiences, as well as, historical facts. The Sister Pact Adventure series was inspired by their two daughters who always keep them both busy. K.M. Parisi resides in Connecticut with his wife and two daughters.

www.ingramcontent.com/pod-product-compliance
Lightning Source LLC
Chambersburg PA
CBHW071520030726
47593CB00003B/1350